Sports Illustrated KIDS

BASKETBALL RECORDS SMASHED!

by Brendan Flynn

CAPSTONE PRESS
a capstone imprint

Published by Capstone Press, an imprint of Capstone
1710 Roe Crest Drive, North Mankato, Minnesota 56003
capstonepub.com

Library of Congress Cataloging-in-Publication Data
Names: Flynn, Brendan, author.
Title: Basketball records smashed! / by Brendan Flynn.
Description: North Mankato : Capstone Press, [2024] | Series: Sports illustrated kids. Record smashers | Includes bibliographical references and index. | Audience: Ages 9–11 | Audience: Grades 4–6 | Summary: "Basketball is filled with great plays from strong players—like Russell Westbrook's record-breaking triple-doubles in 2021 and Sue Bird and Diana Taurasi's hard-to-beat Olympic gold medals. In this Sports Illustrated Kids book, young readers can experience these exciting moments and other record-breaking achievements in basketball. Fast-paced and fact-filled, this collection of record smashers will delight sports fans with thrilling feats in basketball"—Provided by publisher.
Identifiers: LCCN 2023000023 (print) | LCCN 2023000024 (ebook) | ISBN 9781669049937 (hardcover) | ISBN 9781669049890 (pdf) | ISBN 9781669049913 (kindle edition) | ISBN 9781669049920 (epub)
Subjects: LCSH: Basketball—Records—United States—Juvenile literature. | Basketball—United States—History—Juvenile literature.
Classification: LCC GV885.55 .F549 2024 (print) | LCC GV885.55 (ebook) | DDC 796.323/6406—dc23/eng/20230112
LC record available at https://lccn.loc.gov/2023000023
LC ebook record available at https://lccn.loc.gov/2023000024

Editorial Credits
Editor: Ericka Smith; Designer: Terri Poburka; Media Researcher: Svetlana Zhurkin; Production Specialist: Katy LaVigne

Image Credits
Alamy: Universal Images Group North America, 4; Associated Press: Ben Margot, 21, Eric Gay, cover (front), File/Paul Vathis, 8, Warren M. Winterbottom, 7; Getty Images: Andy Lyons, 11, Corbis/Tim Clayton, 13, Doug Pensinger, 24, Ezra Shaw, 5, Jamie Squire, 15, NBAE/Bill Baptist, 23, NBAE/Jeff Haynes, 16, 17, NBAE/Ned Dishman, 12, NBAE/Noah Graham, 9, 14, NBAE/Scott Cunningham, 19, 20, NBAE/Tim Heitman, 27, 28–29, Thearon W. Henderson, 25; Shutterstock: EFKS, cover (back), krissikunterbunt (fireworks), cover and throughout, pixssa (cracked background), 1 and throughout; Sports Illustrated: Manny Millan, 10

TABLE OF CONTENTS

Words in **bold** are in the glossary.

SHOOTING HOOPS

Basketball was invented in 1891 by a teacher in Massachusetts named James Naismith. He created a fun game his students could play in the winter. They shot a ball at a peach basket.

James Naismith

FACT

The Basketball Hall of Fame in Springfield, Massachusetts, is named after Naismith. Many record breakers are honored there.

Basketball has changed a lot since then! Today, millions play basketball around the world. And the best players have set some amazing records!

THE UNSTOPPABLE "WILT THE STILT"

Wilt Chamberlain had a great nickname. Fans called him "Wilt the Stilt" because he was so tall. At 7 feet, 1 inch (2.2 meters), he towered over his **rivals**. He holds many National Basketball Association (NBA) records. One of his records might never be broken.

Chamberlain jumping for a shot

On March 2, 1962, Chamberlain's Philadelphia Warriors were playing the New York Knicks. By halftime, Chamberlain had 41 points. And he just kept scoring. By the end of the game, he had 100 points—an NBA record!

Teammates and fans congratulate Chamberlain on his 100-point game.

FACT

When Chamberlain scored 100 points during that game against the Knicks, he broke his own record. He'd scored 78 points during a game in December 1961.

In 2006, Kobe Bryant scored 81 points in a game. That's the closest anyone has come to Chamberlain's record.

Kobe Bryant shooting a free throw

GOING FOR GOLD

Sue Bird and Diana Taurasi are basketball **legends**. They both won championships at the University of Connecticut. Then, they went on to play in the Women's National Basketball Association (WNBA). But their best was yet to come.

Diana Taurasi

Sue Bird

FACT

Bird and Taurasi were starters on the University of Connecticut's 2002 national championship team.

In 2021, Bird and Taurasi led Team USA to an Olympic gold medal. It was the fifth gold for each of them. Several players have four Olympic gold medals. But Bird and Taurasi topped them all by winning five.

Taurasi during the 2021 gold-medal game

Taurasi (left) and Bird with their fifth gold medals

THREE-POINT THRILLER

Klay Thompson is a great shooter. When he gets an open shot from behind the three-point line, look out! He usually buries it.

Thompson (right) shooting a three-pointer

On October 29, 2018, Thompson smashed the NBA record for three-pointers in one game. That day, his Golden State Warriors faced the Chicago Bulls. By halftime, Thompson had made 10 three-pointers. He was red-hot! His teammates kept setting him up with open shots. And he kept scoring!

Thompson finished with 14 three-pointers! He beat his teammate Stephen Curry's record of 13 three-pointers.

Thompson celebrating 14 three-pointers

TRIPLE-DOUBLE TROUBLE

A triple-double is a big **feat** in basketball. Usually, it means a player has at least 10 points, 10 rebounds, and 10 **assists**.

Russell Westbrook gets a lot of triple-doubles. On May 10, 2021, he was having a great night playing for the Washington Wizards. During the fourth quarter, he grabbed a rebound. It looked like an ordinary play. But it smashed a triple-double record.

Westbrook jumping for a rebound

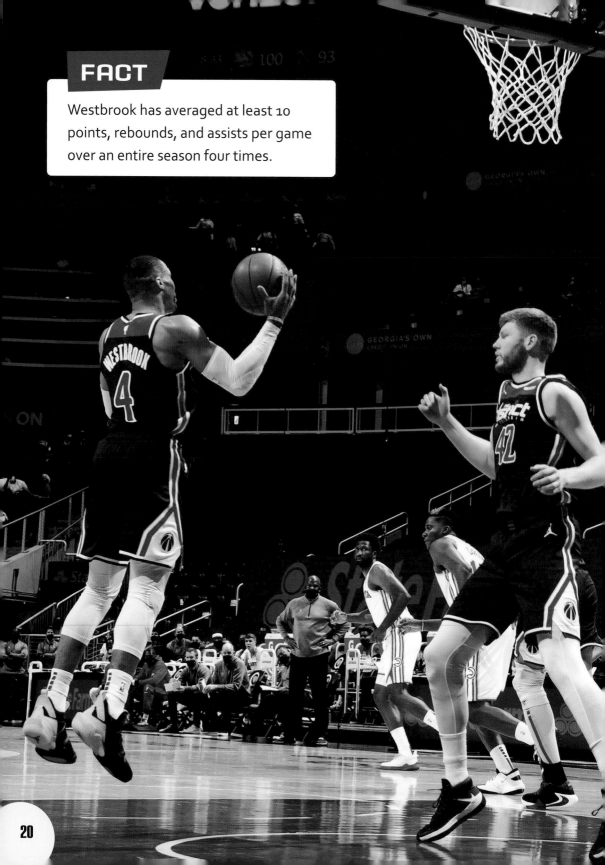

Westbrook has averaged at least 10 points, rebounds, and assists per game over an entire season four times.

When the game ended, Westbrook had 28 points, 13 rebounds, and 21 assists. That gave him 182 triple-doubles in his career. He broke Oscar Robertson's 47-year-old record!

Westbrook celebrating 182 triple-doubles

BIG WINNERS

During the 1995–96 season, the Chicago Bulls were on fire! Michael Jordan was in his **prime**. He had plenty of great teammates too. That year, the Bulls went 72–10. That was the most wins during the regular NBA season.

FACT

The Los Angeles Lakers held the previous record. They went 69–13 during the 1971–72 season.

Jordan shooting a reverse layup

But records are made to be broken. Twenty years later, the Golden State Warriors had 69 wins late in the season. There were just four games left to play in the regular season.

Could they smash the Bulls' record? Yes! The Warriors won every single game. They ended the 2015–16 season with a 73–9 record—the best in NBA history.

Draymond Green of the Warriors shooting a layup in a 2015 game

Andre Iguodala of the Warriors taking a shot during a 2016 game

LIZ SIZZLES

On July 17, 2018, the Dallas Wings faced the New York Liberty. Nobody knew it, but WNBA history was about to be made.

Wings center Liz Cambage was hard to defend. At 6 feet, 8 inches (2 m), she **dominated** close to the basket. And she could shoot three-pointers.

Cambage taking a shot during the 2018 game against the Liberty

Cambage (8) celebrating 53 points with her team

That night, Cambage shot the ball 22 times. She made 17 of those shots. That included 4 three-pointers. She also hit 15 free throws.

Cambage finished the game with 53 points. She smashed Riquna Williams's 2013 record of 51 points in one game!

GLOSSARY

assist (uh-SIST)—a pass that leads to a score by a teammate

dominate (DAH-muh-nayt)—to rule; in sports, a team or person dominates if they win more or play better than others

feat (FEET)—an achievement that requires great courage, skill, or strength

legend (LEJ-uhnd)—someone who is among the best in what they do

prime (PRYME)—the best years of an athlete's career

rival (RYE-vuhl)—someone whom a person competes against

READ MORE

Berglund, Bruce. *Baseball Records Smashed!* North Mankato, MN: Capstone, 2024.

Mattern, Joanne. *Sue Bird*. Lake Elmo, MN: Focus Readers, 2022.

Smith, Elliott. *Basketball's Greatest Myths and Legends*. North Mankato, MN: Capstone, 2023.

INTERNET SITES

Basketball Reference
basketball-reference.com

Naismith Memorial Basketball Hall of Fame
hoophall.com

WNBA
wnba.com

INDEX

ABOUT THE AUTHOR

Brendan Flynn is a San Francisco resident and an author of numerous children's books. In addition to writing about sports, Flynn also enjoys competing in triathlons, Scrabble tournaments, and chili cook-offs.